ANIMAL SNOOPS

The Wondrous World of Wildlife Spies

Peter Christie

Illustrations by
Cat MacInnes

annick press
toronto + new york + vancouver

For Hannah, Laura, and cousin Katherine
champion snoops

Annick Press Ltd.

Edited and copyedited by Elizabeth McLean
Proofread by Paula Ayer
Cover and interior design by Matt Heximer & Susan Lepard at 10four design group
Cover and interior illustrations by Cat MacInnes

We acknowledge the support of the Canada Council for the Arts, the Ontario Arts Council, and the Government of Canada through the Book Publishing Industry Development Program (BPIDP) for our publishing activities.

ONTARIO ARTS COUNCIL
CONSEIL DES ARTS DE L'ONTARIO

Cataloging in Publication

Christie, Peter, 1962-
        Animal snoops : the wondrous world of
wildlife spies / by Peter Christie ; illustrations by Cat MacInnes.

Includes bibliographical references and index.
ISBN 978-1-55451-216-4 (pbk.).—ISBN 978-1-55451-217-1 (bound)

9200

        1. Animal intelligence. 2. Animal behavior. I. MacInnes, Cat II. Title.

QL785.C556 2010   j591.5'13   C2009-905775-1

Printed and bound in China

Published in the U.S.A. by
Annick Press (U.S.) Ltd.

Distributed in Canada by
Firefly Books Ltd.
66 Leek Crescent
Richmond Hill, ON
L4B 1H1

Distributed in the U.S.A. by
Firefly Books (U.S.) Inc.
P.O. Box 1338
Ellicott Station
Buffalo, NY 14205

Visit our website at www.annickpress.com

TABLE OF CONTENTS

PRESENTING:
THE BIRD-BRAINED BURGLAR BUST

The house in Memphis, Tennessee, sat empty: the coast was clear for a robbery. Quickly and secretively, the three young burglars checked the windows and doors and found a way in. They piled up computers, DVD players, and other electronic equipment.

The thieves talked as they worked, paying no attention to the parrot, nearly motionless in its cage. Only when the crooks were ready to make their getaway did the bird finally pipe up. "JJ," it said plainly. "JJ, JJ."

Marshmallow—a six-year-old green parrot— had been quietly eavesdropping. And the private-eye parrot had learned a thing or two, including the nickname of one of the robbers: J.J.

The burglars fled but soon realized that the parrot knew too much. "They were afraid the bird would stool on them," said Billy Reilly, a local police officer. When the thieves returned to the crime scene to nab the bird, police captured them.

Parrot

Pet parrots may listen in to mimic humans, but for wild creatures, eavesdropping can be a matter of survival.

The Memphis crooks hadn't counted on Marshmallow's talents as an eavesdropper. Why would they? Few people imagine that animals can be highly skilled spies and snoops. Yet nature is filled with them.

More and more, scientists are discovering that creatures—from bugs to baboons—are experts at watching, listening, and prying into the lives of other animals. While Marshmallow's eavesdropping helped to foil human criminals, wild spies work for their own benefit. Spying can be the best or fastest way to find food or a mate, or get early warning of a predator.

Until recently, researchers preferred to think of communication between animals as similar to two people talking privately. But wildlife sounds and signals are often loud or bright enough that it is easy for others to listen in. It's like having conversations on Facebook that every one of your friends—and maybe some of your enemies—can read.

Animal messages are often detected by audiences that were not meant to get wind of them. Hungry gopher snakes, for example, use foot-drumming signals between kangaroo rats to locate a snaky snack. Female chickadees listen in on singing contests of territorial males when choosing a mate.

Biologists call it eavesdropping. It sounds sneaky, but it works well. And some animals are doubly sneaky, changing their behavior when they expect to be overheard. The animal communication network is far more complicated than researchers used to believe.

Drumming up dinner! A hungry gopher snake follows the foot thumps of communicating kangaroo rats.

Gopher Snake

In nature, prying eyes and ears are everywhere.

The stakes in wild spy games are high. Eavesdropping can determine whether animals mate, find a home, or enjoy a sneaky life instead of meeting sudden death. It can reveal whom they should trust and even affect the evolution of songs and signals.

Naturally clever secret agents learn things from snooping that help them survive and pass their genes to the next generation. It's one more tool that crafty creatures use to understand the world around them.

THE SPY WHO LOVED ME: SPYING AND PRYING TO FIND A MATE

CHAPTER 1

Chacma Baboon

On the grassy floodplains of the Okavango Delta, in the deepening green of an African evening, a young chacma baboon sat watching the members of his troop. While some played or groomed one another, the dominant males—the baboon big shots—each followed a female that was ready to mate. They stuck close, determined to keep other males away.

The young baboon paid careful attention to the couples. He was a subordinate male, meaning he was well down the social ladder. He had no status to challenge other males, and it was lonely at the bottom.

But the silent baboon wasn't brooding over his bad luck. He was spying—quietly listening to the intimate exchanges of the baboon pairs. The males uttered distinctive grunts to the females, and the

Spying on baboon couples might help a young male find a female alone, giving him a chance to mate.

females responded with a high, almost musical call. From these nuptial noises, the young eavesdropper tracked each couple.

Now he heard a sound that excited him: a familiar grunt over here and the matching call over there—a pair had become separated. The young male jumped into action. If he could reach the female before her top-dog male located her, he might sneak a secret mating.

For some animals—such as low-ranking male baboons—spying on couples can improve their own mating chances. By eavesdropping on courtship noises and displays, sneaky creatures increase the odds of having young and passing on their genes.

Male European robins eavesdrop to know when a neighboring female feels neglected.

European Robin

Among birds, male European robins spy on robin pairs that court and nest in the hedgerows and gardens of Europe. When it's time to lay eggs, a female robin gets her mate's attention by cheeping a loud begging cry. The male responds by delivering gifts—squishy caterpillars, grubs, and other romantic delicacies—and often the two will mate.

Neighboring males listen in. If a female doesn't get her treat quickly, she cheeps more frantically. A noisy female means her mate isn't paying enough attention. For the snoop next door, it may mean the time is right for a secret encounter. He may offer the neglected female a food gift and try to father some of her young.

Male Uganda kob may think they're hot stuff, but females often simply copy other females to choose a mate.

Animals that spy for a chance to reproduce are not always male; sometimes females snoop in mating matters. In the flat scrublands of central Africa, for instance, females of two kinds of antelope, Uganda kob and Kafue lechwe, get especially nosy during the breeding season.

The male antelope gather on traditional mating grounds—called leks—to attract the attention of females. Leks offer a kind of one-stop shopping for females to compare suitors.

But scientists say the females don't just compare the males they see; they also snoop on the choices of other females. By sniffing the soil, these antelope detectives can tell which area has had the most female interest, because females urinate during courtship. The male that occupies that territory will be the most popular mate on the lek.

Size matters. Female convict cichlids spy when two males meet to determine which one measures up.

The sniff test is so important to females that biologists have been able to change mate choices by moving urine-soaked soil from one spot to another.

Even after pairing up, female convict cichlids keep their sly eyes open to see how their males compare. These colorful, aggressive little fish live in the streams and lakes of Central America, and many people keep them in aquariums. Males and females usually form lasting pairs, and both parents raise their young.

But in the world of cichlids, bigger is better, and females prefer larger males. With no measuring tape, females size up males by watching them square off with rivals in territory disputes. Researchers say that more than half the females who see other males outsize their mates will abandon the relationship to hook up with the bigger male.

NOSY ABOUT PEEING CONTESTS

Female pygmy lorises know when to stick their noses into others' business. Many of them do just that to find the best mate.

Lorises are small, slow-moving primates that live in the trees of Southeast Asia. They're active at night, and very territorial. Males mark their territories with strong-smelling urine. Neighboring males may try to claim the same area or show their higher status by urinating over a rival's mark in a kind of peeing contest.

Although these toilet-time quarrels are a male–male competition, snoopy females often check the evidence. Their noses are able to sniff out the winner: the male whose scent mark is on top. The females appear to prefer the loris who peed last.

Pygmy Slow Loris

A peeing contest isn't child's play. This baby pygmy slow loris must grow up to sniff out a champion.

CHAPTER 2

THE HUNGRY SPY:
SPYING AND PRYING PREDATORS

The path home was one the eastern chipmunk had traveled a hundred times before: under the ferns to the narrow tunnel into his burrow. The small animal ran briskly through the quiet Pennsylvania forest.

Suddenly, a flash and a sting. The startled chipmunk jumped. Dried leaves scattered. A sharp pain seared his haunches. Scrambling away, he glimpsed the motionless length of a timber rattlesnake.

The ambush had succeeded. The deadly serpent had lain coiled and still for many hours, waiting. Even now, after striking, the snake was in no hurry. She would track down the chipmunk's lifeless body after her venom had done its work.

The detective toolkit of a timber rattlesnake includes a tongue that can detect the faintest scent of its prey.

Patience is among the most practiced skills of a rattlesnake. Snooping is another. Before choosing an ambush site, timber rattlesnakes study the habits of their prey. Using their highly sensitive, flickering tongues, the snakes use scent clues to reveal the routines of rodents and other tasty animals.

Their tongues are so remarkable that they also pry into the hunting habits of other rattlesnakes. Scenting the difference between a recently fed rattlesnake and a hungry one, they use the clues to hide where another snake has dined and the hunting is likely to be successful.

For many animals, snooping and spying can mean the difference between a full stomach and starvation. Some creatures, like the rattlesnake, spy on the habits of their prey. Others intercept private communication—and think of the signals as a call to supper.

Photinus fireflies, for instance, broadcast their mating messages with a light show. These plant-eating beetles flash luminescent abdomens to wow potential mates on warm North American summer nights.

A bigger relative is named *Photuris*. They also blink biological tail lights during courtship, but are not always looking for a mate. These fireflies are predators that eat their smaller *Photinus* cousins. They spy on their blinking prey and follow the flashing beacon to a nighttime meal.

In the still-frigid early spring of northern Europe, a male moor frog begins his tuneless chorus: *Waug, waug, waug.*

Not minding that the ice has barely loosed its grip on the pond edge, the frog has emerged from wintering beneath marsh-bottom muck. He's all set to attract female moor frogs the moment they wake from chilly months of sleep.

Waug, waug, waug... WH**A**M!

A flashing **Photinus** firefly looks good to his mate—but he looks delicious to his **Photuris** cousin!

For white storks,
the songs of
courting moor frogs
are dinner music.

With a lightning strike, the long, lance-like bill of a white stork jabs through the marsh grass and snatches up the singing frog. In an instant, the tireless music-maker becomes the dinner of a spy.

White storks are master eavesdroppers. They rely on the songs of moor frogs to guide them when they're hunting. The birds are so skilful that they can stealthily follow frog sounds to within two or three strides of an unsuspecting singer.

By placing himself between a honeybee and a flower, a red-spotted crab spider nabs lunch.

Crab Spider

Some spies can intercept signals sent by plants. Bright flowers invite bees and other animals to come for a meal of pollen or nectar (and to pollinate the plants at the same time). Scientists believe that the most symmetrical flowers— where each half mirrors the other like two sides of a face—help bees and birds recognize them as healthy, with top-quality pollen and nectar.

But crab spiders are deadly spies: they love to eat honeybees and know all about this flower–bee communication system. These sneaky spiders build their bee-trapping webs next to good-looking, symmetrical blooms that bees are more likely to visit.

DEEP SECRETS OVERHEARD

Tick, tick, creak.

In the eerie, deep-water gloom off the coast of Norway, an enormous sperm whale makes mysterious noises before it abruptly rakes its toothy mouth through a school of swimming squid.

Scientists believe the whale is using echolocation—in the same way bats use echoes of their ultrasonic chirps to "see" in the dark. The whale's ticks and creaks help it zero in on prey.

But the sounds may also help distant sperm whales to find a good meal. The whales' echolocation sounds travel far, farther than the length of Manhattan Island. Sly sperm whales may eavesdrop to learn where another whale is hunting successfully, and drop by for lunch.

Sperm Whale

Sperm whales eavesdrop on the feeding sounds of other whales to find a meal.

LIVE AND LET DIE:
SPYING AND PRYING TO STAY ALIVE

Gunther's Dik-dik

The tiny antelope jerked his head up to listen.

He was a Gunther's dik-dik, a miniature antelope no larger than a Labrador dog. The tall grasses of the East African savannah surrounded him like a curtain: he was well hidden from leopards and hyenas, but predators were also concealed from him. Through the chattering of birds and insects, the dik-dik recognized a familiar sound: *Gwaa, gwaa, gwaa.*

The insistent cry had an electric effect on the dik-dik. He leaped and bolted through the grass. The fleeing animal glimpsed the source of the sound—on a nearby tree sat a white-bellied go-away bird, sentinel of the savannah. Beyond it, barely visible above the grass, were the large black ears of a hunting wild dog.

Go-away Bird

Go-away birds are known for their noisy alarm call; the *gwaa* is thought by some to sound like a person shouting "g'away." These social birds feed together in chattering groups. A loud, urgent *gwaa* cry is a signal to other go-away birds that an eagle, wild dog, or other predator has been spotted nearby.

Many of these dangerous hunters also eat dik-diks. The wary antelopes use every trick in the book to avoid becoming a meal— including eavesdropping on go-away bird communication. Unable to see far on the grassy savannah, dik-diks rely on the birds, which spot approaching predators from treetop lookouts.

LOOK CLOSER

Costumes

SURVEILLANCE TARGETS

Galápagos Marine Iguana

For many animals, spying is a life-and-death business. Creatures that catch warning signals meant for others may stay one step ahead of enemies. Iguanas on the Galápagos Islands, for instance, keep their ears open even though they never utter a sound themselves.

Galápagos marine iguanas feed on algae in the sea. When they're basking on rocks along the shore, young iguanas are a prime target for hungry Galápagos hawks. Another favorite hawk meal is the Galápagos mockingbird, but these birds have something to say about it: a distinctive chirp warns other mockingbirds a hawk is approaching. Marine iguanas eavesdrop on mockingbird conversations. They can tell the alarm from other songs and calls and will dash for cover when they hear it.

A Galápagos marine iguana may be silent, but he's all ears when it comes to mockingbird calls.

Some animal snoops are born recognizing the warning signals of different creatures; others, such as bonnet macaques, have to learn. These monkeys of southern India often pal around with langur monkeys. Langurs are good lookouts, and macaques will quickly scramble up a tree when they overhear a langur warning cry— as long as the macaques have learned the correct langur language.

Scientists say bonnet macaques at one animal reserve respond to recorded Nilgiri langur alarm shrieks but are slower to flee after a similar cry by Hanuman langurs—which would rarely be seen there. Farther north, only Hanuman langurs are common and bonnet macaques there have learned the opposite langur language. They jump at the sound of Hanuman warnings but are less bothered by Nilgiri cries.

Bonnet macaques will escape up a tree when they overhear a langur warning cry.

Eavesdropping on the alarm signals of other animals is useful, but spying on predators directly also has advantages. Geometrid moths, for instance, are slow, night-flying moths that can be easily overtaken by hunting bats. To make up for their sluggish speed, the moths have espionage skills—they can track bat radar.

Many moths are stone deaf, but geometrid moths have ears that tune into the ultrasonic frequency bats use when navigating by echolocation. Not only can they hear a bat approaching, geometrid moths can also tell how close it is. If a bat is nearer than two bus lengths away, a moth will begin evasive zigzag flying. Closer than one bus length and the moth folds its wings and plummets to the ground, where the bat won't follow.

Geometrid Moth

A geometrid moth can avoid bats on the hunt, with its ears tuned to their echolocation signals.

POP AND STOP

The seagrass is alive with the sound of music.

Singing fish—male Gulf toadfish—
are performing their bizarre courtship
serenade in the azure waters off the
coast of Florida: *Grunt, grunt, trrrrrrt*.
It's a song only a female toadfish
could like... unless an
appreciative bottlenose
dolphin is also in the
audience.

Dolphins love to eat toadfish, and they eavesdrop on the singing fish to find their dinner. But the dolphins aren't the only spies in the sea: the toadfish spy on the dolphins, too. Dolphins make a low-frequency "pop" sound when they use sonar to reveal toadfish hidden under dense seagrass. The fish listen for popping from hunting dolphins, and stop singing when the sound gets near.

Gulf Toadfish

Gulf toadfish know when to stay silent— and safe—by listening in on the sonar of bottlenose dolphins.

SIZING HIM UP:
SPYING AND PRYING
INTO ANIMAL
CONTESTS

4

Capuchin Monkey

Snooping around helps a white-faced capuchin monkey tell friend from foe.

The dense forests of Costa Rica can be shadowy and mysterious—the perfect place for spies to hang out.

And one spy—a white-faced capuchin monkey—was doing exactly that. He was dangling from tree branches, quietly snooping on other monkeys as they quarreled or groomed one another. The capuchin's mission was clear: he was spying to learn which of his friends might also be friendly with his foes.

White-faced capuchin monkeys are known for their remarkably human-like characteristics: a large brain, a varied diet, and... a habit of sometimes ganging together to bully and attack others they don't like. Sometimes these group fights are deadly.

By watching social monkey business, capuchins can learn which troop mates would make the best friends to have around when a fight breaks out. A low-ranking male often wants to team up with a stronger, dominant male, but not with one who is also the buddy of an enemy. They might both turn against him in a brawl.

Clever spying could help the capuchin pick the winning side—and scientists say that few non-human creatures are capable of such a trick.

In times of war, a little espionage goes a long way. Before picking a fight over food, mates, or territory, some creatures check out a rival by spying on his performance in battle.

Siamese fighting fish seem to be natural warriors. In Southeast Asia, where these fish live, people sometimes put male fighting fish together in tanks and gamble on their fights. Contests often end in the death of one of the combatants.

Other male fighting fish are also fans of violent fish bouts. The males watch rivals battle to see how tough the opponents are. Afterward, they avoid challenging the winning fighter but confidently attack the loser.

Siamese
Fighting Fish

Like human boxers, Siamese fighting fish check out the competition by watching others fight.

Sometimes females like to spy when two males duke it out. A fight outcome can say a lot about a male's suitability as a mate. Female domestic canaries, for instance, like to watch when males scrap over food at a birdcage seed dispenser.

Scientists say female canaries may choose a mate based on these brief battles—but in an unexpected way: the females prefer the *losers*. Researchers believe the females may want to avoid males that could be dangerously aggressive and hurt them. "Winning" by losing appears rare in the animal world, but female Japanese quail also prefer defeated quail to the dangerous champions of male–male quail fights.

Domestic Canary

Tough guys don't always win! Female canaries watch males fight, but prefer the losers as mates.

CLAW AWE

In a watery Texas ditch, two male red swamp crayfish raise their scarlet pincers and square off in a battle for territory. Within moments, the larger male pins his rival with a huge claw. The smaller crayfish escapes, but he won't soon forget the lesson of this battle.

Neither will the closet claw-fight fans secretly watching from the sidelines. Although male crayfish contests are, strictly speaking, "a guy thing," female crayfish spy on matches to decide who's hot or not. According to researchers, females have trouble deciding on a mate unless they've seen a claw-to-claw bout—then, they're far more likely to choose the winner.

Red Swamp Crayfish

En garde! When male red swamp crayfish fight, females secretly watch from the sidelines.

CHAPTER 5

THE SNOOPY HOUSE HUNTER:

SPYING AND PRYING TO FIND A HOME

FOR SALE

FOR SALE

As the skies over northern Poland grew lighter, the approaching dawn had an urgent message for the night creatures. Bedtime, said the sunrise. Time to sleep. For an agile woodland flyer called a noctule bat, the message had added pressure: bedtime meant finding a bed.

The bat maneuvered easily through the woods, nabbing moths on the wing. Echolocation helped him to picture objects such as trees and insects in the dark. But noctule bats roost in tree holes and cracks that are difficult to find by echolocation alone. Other tools come in handy— the eavesdropping skills of a spy, for instance, are particularly useful.

Noctule bats live in groups, and they move every few nights to avoid being discovered by snakes and other predators. To find a new roost, the bats must crawl up and down trees, spending valuable time and leaving themselves vulnerable to owls and other night stalkers.

Some bats play it safe by spying. They let others do the exploratory work and then listen for echolocation chirps and other calls as the bats settle down to roost. The eavesdroppers zero in on these sounds to find their way to a cozy bedroom for the day.

Noctule Bat

Noctule bats eavesdrop on the ultrasonic chatter of other bats to find out where they're roosting.

When they're house-hunting, Panama grass anoles spy to see where other anoles settle.

Finding a good home is as important to animals as it is to us: it means safe shelter close to plentiful food. But locating the right place can take a lot of effort—or some crafty snooping.

In the sun-baked scrublands of Panama, Panamanian grass anoles searching for a home are less interested in the rocky, dry landscape than in other grass anoles. Scientists say these small, nosy lizards pay close attention to where other lizards lounge. By spying on fellow anoles, they can avoid bad neighborhoods—places where cicadas and other tasty insects are few and where anole-eating kestrels and other enemies are plentiful.

In the late-summer woodlands of North America, black-throated blue warblers spy on the singing habits of other black-throated blues. The information comes in handy when they're house-hunting the next spring. Most warblers sing after nesting season only if their chicks have survived. Scientists believe the adults may be giving music lessons to the youngsters. Silence after nesting likely means that no eggs hatched, that the chicks starved or died from illness, or that a nest was attacked by predators.

After spending the winter in South and Central America, returning warblers tend to settle where they overheard end-of-season singers the previous year. Even if the forest is too young and shrubby to provide good nesting places or to support enough caterpillars and insects for the warblers to eat, the birds prefer places that *sounded* successful.

Late-summer songs by black-throated blue warblers mean the birds successfully raised their chicks.

Black-Throated Blue Warbler

EGG-CELLENT ESPIONAGE

There she was again—a duck in the "doorway."

The female common goldeneye was poking her head through the opening to a deep tree-hole nest in a northern Quebec forest. Inside, another goldeneye sat quietly on her downy young. As the startled mother glanced up, the visitor flew away. The nesting female had just been visited by a spy.

Some goldeneye females snoop so they can secretly lay eggs in the nests of other females—but these egg-dumpers aren't shirkers. They spy on nests to discover the best moms, making note of who raised young and who suffered nest attacks by squirrels and snakes. A year later, these spies may lay a few of their eggs in tree holes owned by reliably "expert" caregivers.

Goldeneye Duck

Some female common goldeneyes snoop on good mothers, then secretly lay eggs in the other bird's nest.

SPY VS. SPY: TRICKING EAVESDROPPERS

Eastern Gray Squirrel

Some eastern gray squirrels foil spies and would-be robbers by digging fake food caches.

The secret agent glanced around nervously. Enemy eyes were everywhere. She would have to act fast or her stash could be in jeopardy.

In the shadows of a quiet Massachusetts woodlot, she quickly dug a shallow pit, then filled it in. She covered it with leaves and dashed off again. Her hurriedly buried treasure lay safe in its new hiding place.

Or did it?

The agent's identity was no mystery: it was an eastern gray squirrel and her stash was a cache of gathered seeds. Gray squirrels plan ahead by hiding food to retrieve later. But other squirrels and also birds, such as blue jays, spy on gray squirrels to find their secret larders.

Gray squirrels create many caches, so the discovery of one wouldn't be a catastrophic loss, but the squirrels hate to have any loot plundered. That's why they use anti-snoop techniques if they believe their food stashes are in danger.

When gray squirrels overhear blue jay calls, they put less food in each cache. Biologists believe the squirrels know that nearby jays increase the risk that a cache will be found, and try to minimize loss.

But the squirrels have a better way to foil nosy would-be robbers—deception. Gray squirrels dig fake storage holes and cover them up again, with no food inside at all. It's highly sophisticated trickery that scientists say is very rare in the animal world.

Longfin Inshore Squid

For many creatures, spying is essential for mating and survival. For others, avoiding spies is equally important. Longfin inshore squid, for instance, have developed an amazing counter-espionage skill to hide from the prying eyes of enemies.

Like other squid and octopuses, longfin inshore squid can rapidly change color. Using their skin like an electronic billboard, these squid can flash through a rainbow of hues to warn rivals and attract mates.

The problem with jazzy visual messages is that they can also be obvious to snooping sea turtles, seals, and other predators. But the longfin inshore squid has a sneaky solution: a two-layered signaling system. Its skin has an outer layer of light-reflecting cells that contain black, brown, red, orange, and yellow pigments. Squid can hide from enemies by changing the color of this layer to blend in with their surroundings.

At the same time, another layer of cells reflects iridescent green, blue, gold, and silver polarized light. Polarized light is invisible to many animals, including humans. But the squid's eyes can easily see the dazzling broadcasts. Most of its enemies, meanwhile, are blind to the iridescent colors—and to the squid's secret code.

Some animals have to deal with spies and double-crossers that are more of a threat to successful mating than to life and limb. Male Atlantic mollies, for instance, are fish that resort to outright deception to fool other males about which female molly has caught their eye.

Atlantic Mollies

Male Atlantic mollies prefer to keep their real mate choice a secret.

Many male mollies prefer large, fertile females, but some snoops prefer to copy the mate choice of other males. It saves them the effort of sizing up a potential partner themselves. When a courting male becomes aware that a competitor is spying on him, he abruptly shifts his attention to a small, less desirable female. This clever trick diverts spies from the male's true object of affection.

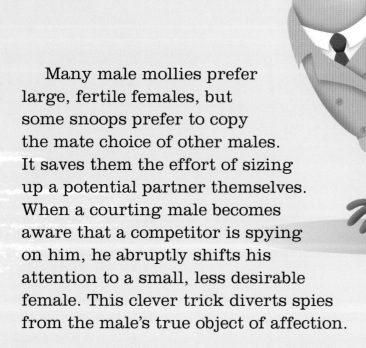

Killer whales that swim in British Columbia's straits come in two types: quiet and chatty. It's not just a matter of personality, though. The preferred menu choice of the chatty whales, known as resident orcas, is salmon. Fish can't hear, so these whales are free to be as talkative as they please.

The quiet whales, known as transient orcas, hunt seals, porpoises, and other marine mammals. These animals can all hear well underwater—and can easily eavesdrop on whales that are too talkative. Researchers say the stealthy transient whales appear to have completely altered their communication style to avoid being detected by their snoopy favorite prey.

Silent but deadly. Some killer whales keep quiet to hunt for eavesdropping seals.

Killer Whale

A FISHY CLOAKING DEVICE

Knife fish really get a charge out of one another—but sometimes that electricity invites danger.

In the murky rivers of South and Central America, male knife fish serenade females using weak electrical pulses. The pulses also help them find their way in the gloom. But predatory electric eels and catfish can detect the low-frequency charges, and eavesdrop on tasty knife fish to hunt them down.

Knife Fish

An ingenious "cloaking" strategy hides the electrical signals of knife fish from predatory catfish and electric eels.

Biologists say many knife fish have an ingenious "cloaking" strategy to prevent spying. They send a second pulse right after the first one. Electricity travels in waves, and the two pulse waves are timed so that when they meet, their high and low points cancel each other out. At a distance, where hungry spies lurk, the telltale electrical signals have disappeared.

CURTAINS:
WHAT NOSY NEIGHBORS KNOW

Mean old Scrooge was in the chimp room.

The man at the primate research center in Louisiana simply refused to give Megan, a teenage chimpanzee, any fruit from his tray. The person was one of eight strangers who tempted Megan with food before holding the tray out of reach.

For social animals, such as chimps, spying is one way to recognize a reliable buddy when you need one.

Chimpanzee

Thank goodness for the others. Humans from a second group showed up afterward, offered the tray, and let Megan take her fill. Go figure! People are such a riddle sometimes.

Megan wasn't the only chimp left to ponder what strange creatures humans are. Four other chimps—Apollo, Kara, Candy, and Jadine—were allowed to spy on this experiment through a special window.

These snoopy apes soon recognized which humans were unkind and which were generous without any direct contact. Meeting the same people later, the observer chimps knew to gesture only to the generous ones, "asking" for food.

For creatures that snoop to find food, spying can be a matter of survival. It's the same for social animals—such as chimps—that spy to learn who they can count on when they're hungry.

Eavesdropping on how others behave may seem sneaky, but it makes sense for animals that live in groups. It's really an important part of being social, and a risk-free way to know which fellow animal to turn to for help. That's vital information when trusting the wrong one can have a deadly ending.

An animal kingdom infiltrated by spies may be a hard place for creatures to keep a secret. And by prying into the lives of animals, scientists have uncovered just how essential eavesdropping can be. Wild snoops are impressive secret agents on a constant mission of survival—whether they're mating or fighting, hunting or hiding, or figuring out who their friends are.

LOOK CLOSER

Costumes

SURVEILLANCE TARGETS

FURTHER READING

Arnosky, Jim. *All about Rattlesnakes*. New York: Scholastic Press, 2002.

Denega, Daniella. *24/7: Science behind the Scenes: Spy Files: The Cold War Pigeon Patrols and Other Animal Spies*. London: Franklin Watts, 2007.

Donovan, Sandra. *Iguanas*. Eustis, FL: Raintree Books, 2003.

Doris, Ellen. *Ornithology (Real Kids/Real Science Books)*. New York: Thames & Hudson, 1994.

Fink-Martin, Patricia A. *Lemurs, Lorises, and Other Lower Primates*. New York: Children's Press, 2000.

Goodall, Jane. *Chimpanzee Family Book*. New York: North-South Books, 1997.

Greenberg, Nicki. *It's True! An Octopus Has Deadly Spit*. Toronto: Annick Press, 2007.

Imbriaco, Alison. *The Sperm Whale: Help Save This Endangered Species!* Berkeley Heights, NJ: Myreportlinks.com, 2008.

Kalman, Bobbie, and Rebecca Sjonger. *Crayfish*. New York: Crabtree, 2006.

Kennett, David. *Killer Whale*. Malvern, Australia: Omnibus Books, 2002.

Landau, Elaine. *True Books: Electric Fish*. New York: Children's Press, 2001.

Mattern, Joanne. *Animals of the Savannah*. New York: Rosen, 2002.

National Geographic Society. *National Geographic Animal Encyclopedia*. Washington, DC: National Geographic Children's Books, 2000.

Presnall, Judith Janda. *Capuchin Monkey Helpers*. Chicago: KidHaven Press, 2003.

Shah, Anup. *The Circle of Life: Wildlife on the African Savannah*. New York: Abrams Books, 2003.

Siamese Fighting Fish. New York: Children's Press, 2002.

Tagliaferro, Linda. *Galapagos Islands*. Minneapolis: Lerner, 2002.

Taylor, Barbara. *Apes and Monkeys*. London: Anness, 2004.

SELECTED BIBLIOGRAPHY

Amy, M., M. Monbureau, C.M. Durand, D. Gomez, M.T. Ry, and G.R. Leboucher. 2008. Female canary mate preferences: differential use of information from two types of male-male interaction. *Animal Behaviour* 76: 971–82.

Aquiloni, L., M. Buřič, and Francesca Gherardi. 2008. Crayfish females eavesdrop on fighting males before choosing the dominant mate. *Current Biology* 18: R462–63.

Betts, M.G., A.S. Hadley, N. Rodenhouse, and J.J. Nocera. 2008. Social information trumps vegetation structure in breeding-site selection by a migrant songbird. *Proceedings of the Royal Society* B 275: 2257–63.

Clark, R.W. 2007. Public information for solitary foragers: timber rattlesnakes use conspecific chemical cues to select ambush sites. *Behavioral Ecology* 18: 487–90.

Crockford, C., R.M. Wittig, R.M. Seyfarth, and D.L. Cheney. 2007. Baboons eavesdrop to deduce mating opportunities. *Animal Behaviour* 73: 885–90.

de Crespigny, F.E.C., and D.J. Hosken. Sexual selection: signals to die for. *Current Biology* 17: R853–54.

Deecke, V.B., J.K.B. Ford, and P.J.B. Slater. 2005. The vocal behaviour of mammal-eating killer whales: communicating with costly calls. *Animal Behaviour* 69: 395–405.

Deutsch, J.C., and R.J.C. Nefdt. 1992. Olfactory cues influence female choice in two lek-breeding antelopes. *Nature* 356: 596–98.

Dzieweczynski, T.L., R.L. Earley, T.M. Green, and W.J. Rowland. 2005. Audience effect is context dependent in Siamese fighting fish, *Betta splendens. Behavioral Ecology* 16: 1025–30.

Fisher, H.S., R.R. Swaisgood, and H. Fitch-Snyder. 2003. Countermarking by male pygmy lorises *(Nycticebus pygmaeus)*: do females use odor cues to select mates with high competitive ability? *Behavioral Ecology Sociobiology* 53:123–30.

Igaune, K., I. Krams, T. Krama, and J. Bobkova. 2008. White storks *Ciconia ciconia* eavesdrop on mating calls of moor frogs *Rana arvalis. Journal of Avian Biology* 39: 229–32.

Kiester, A.R. 1979. Conspecifics as cues: a mechanism for habitat selection in the Panamanian grass anole *(Anolis auratus). Behavioural Ecology and Sociobiology* 5: 323–30.

Lea, A.J., J.P. Barrera, L.M. Tom, and D.T. Blumstein. 2008. Heterospecific eavesdropping in a nonsocial species. *Behavioral Ecology* 19: 1041–46.

Madsen, P.T., M. Wahlberg, and B. Møhl. 2002. Male sperm whale *(Physeter macrocephalus)* acoustics in a high-latitude habitat: implications for echolocation and communication. *Behavioural Ecology and Sociobiology* 53: 31–41.

Mäthger, L.M., and Roger T. Hanlon. 2006. Anatomical basis for camouflaged polarized light communication in squid. *Biology Letters* 2: 494–96.

Perry, S., H. Clark Barrett, and J.H. Manson. 2004. White-faced capuchin monkeys show triadic awareness in their choice of allies. *Animal Behaviour* 67: 165–70.

Plath, M., S. Richter, R. Tiedemann, and I. Schlupp. 2008. Male fish deceive competitors about mating preferences. *Current Biology* 18: 1138–41.

Pöysä, H. 2006. Public information and conspecific nest parasitism in goldeneyes: targeting safe nests by parasites. *Behavioral Ecology* 17: 459–65.

Ramakrishnan, U., and R.G. Coss. 2000. Recognition of heterospecific alarm vocalizations by bonnet macaques (*Macaca radiata*). *Journal of Comparative Psychology* 114: 3–12.

Remage-Healey, L., D.P. Nowacek, and A.H. Bass. 2006. Dolphin foraging sounds suppress calling and elevate stress hormone levels in a prey species, the Gulf toadfish. *The Journal of Experimental Biology* 209: 4444–51.

Ruczynski, I., E.K.V. Kalko, and B.M. Siemers. 2008. The sensory basis of roost finding in a forest bat, *Nyctalus noctula*. *The Journal of Experimental Biology* 210: 3607–15.

Rydell, J., N. Skals, A. Surlykke, and M. Svensson. 1997. Hearing and bat defence in geometrid winter moths. *Proceedings of the Royal Society* B 264: 83–88.

Steele, M.A., S.L. Halkin, P.D. Smallwood, T.J. Mckenna, K. Mitsopoulos, and M. Beam. 2008. Cache protection strategies of a scatter-hoarding rodent: do tree squirrels engage in behavioural deception? *Animal Behaviour* 75: 705–14.

Stoddart, P., and M.R. Markham. 2008. Signal cloaking by electric fish. *BioScience* 58: 415–25.

Subiaul, F., J. Vonk, S. Okamoto-Barth, and J. Barth. 2008. Do chimpanzees learn reputation by observation? Evidence from direct and indirect experience with generous and selfish strangers. *Animal Cognition* 11: 611–23.

Tobias, J.A., and N. Seddon. 2002. Female begging in European robins: do neighbors eavesdrop for extrapair copulations? *Behavioral Ecology* 13: 637–42.

van Breukelen, N.A., and M. Draud. 2002. The roles of male size and female eavesdropping in divorce in the monogamous convict cichlid (*Archocentrus nigrofasciatus*, Cichlidae). *Behaviour* 142: 1029–41.

Vitousek, M.N., J.S. Adelman, N.C. Gregory, and J.J.H. St Clair. 2007. Heterospecific alarm call recognition in a non-vocal reptile. *Biology Letters* 3: 632–34.

Wignall, A.E., A.M. Heiling, K. Cheng, and M.E. Herberstein. 2006. Flower symmetry preferences in honeybees and their crab spider predators. *Ethology* 112: 510–18.

INDEX

ACKNOWLEDGMENTS

I would like to thank Professor Daniel Mennill at the Department of Biological Sciences, University of Windsor, Ontario, and Noah Zylstra for their review of the material in this book and for their comments and suggestions. I would also like to thank Cat MacInnes, Matt Heximer and Sue Lepard, Elizabeth McLean, and Paula Ayer for their fine work putting this together. And, as always, thanks to Hannah, Laura, and Priscilla for their support and patience.

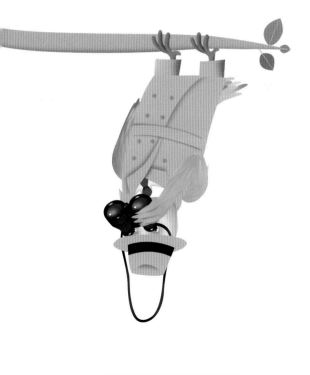

PHOTO CREDITS

Peter Christie is a science writer and author with a lasting fascination for animals and the remarkable things they do. His earlier books for children, ***Well-schooled Fish and Feathered Bandits*** (2006) and ***Naturally Wild Musicians*** (2007), explore other amazing discoveries from the science of animal behavior. ***The Curse of Akkad*** (2008) describes the history of catastrophic climate changes through human history. Peter lives with his wife and two young daughters in Kingston, Ontario.

Cat MacInnes's illustrations have appeared in publications including *3x3*, *Lürzer's Archive: 200 Best Illustrators Worldwide*, and *Typotastic*. She lives near Melbourne, Australia.